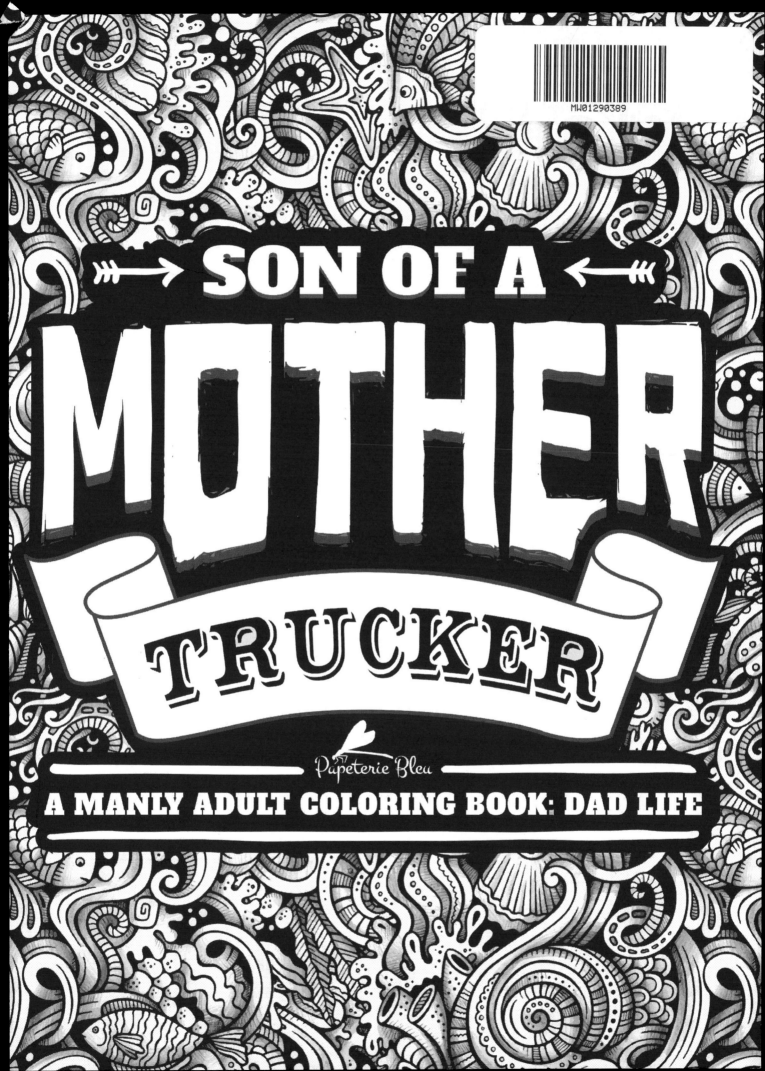

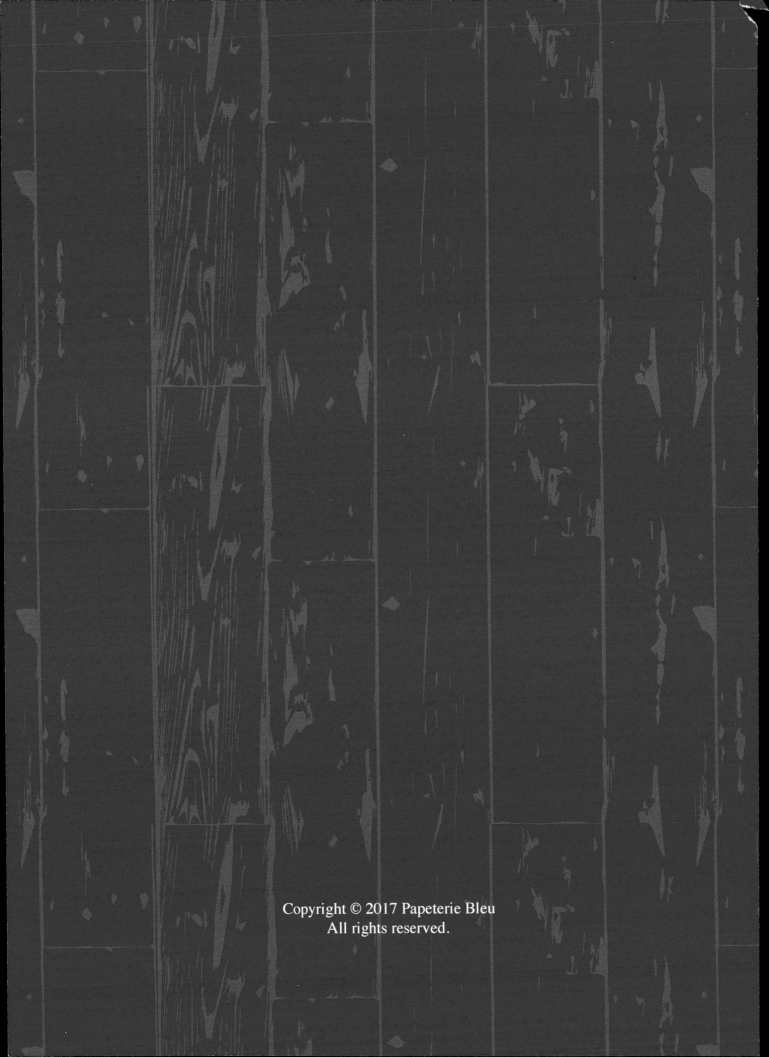

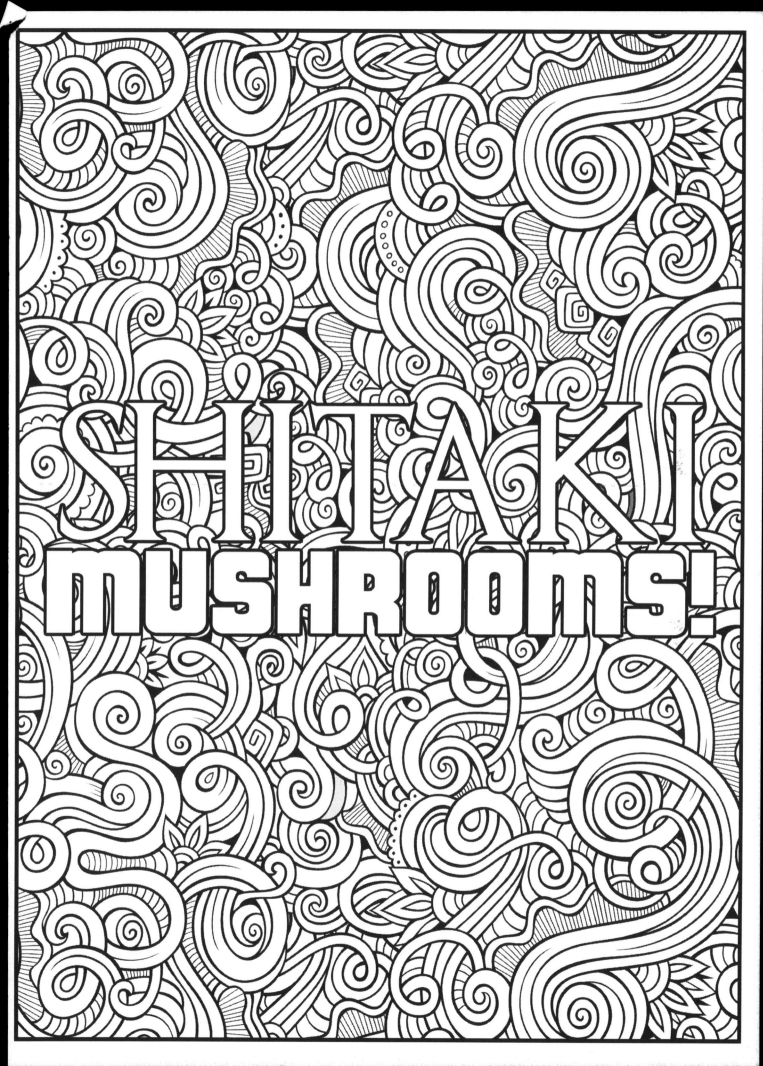

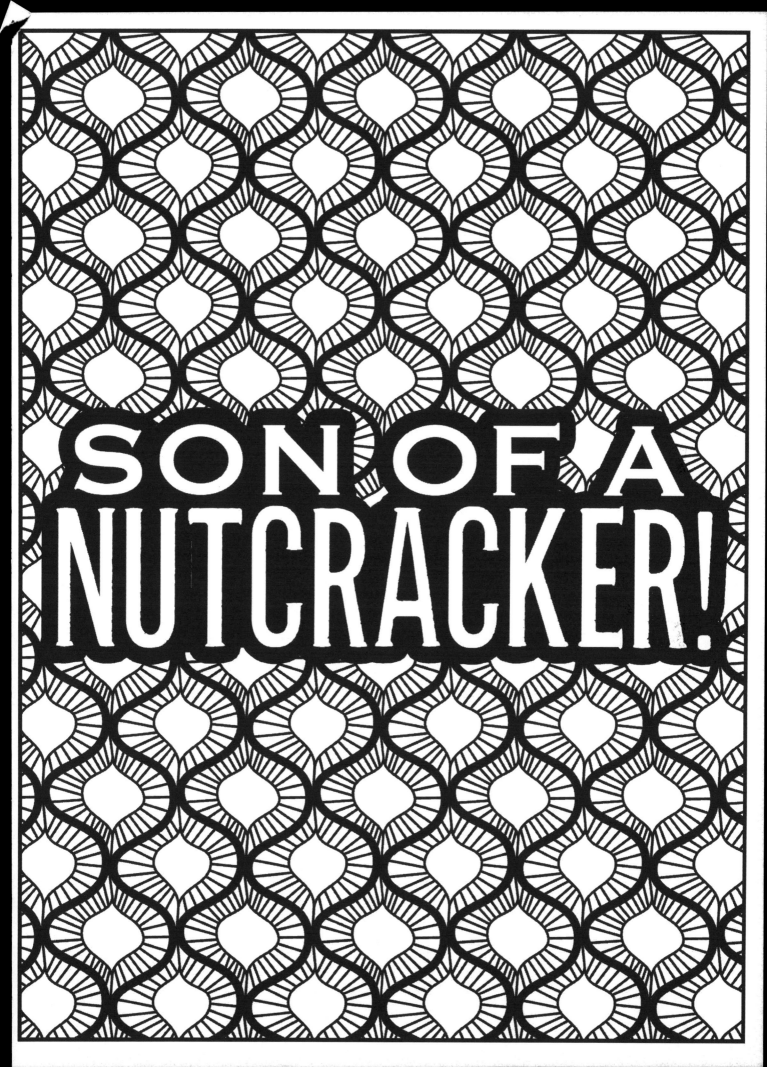

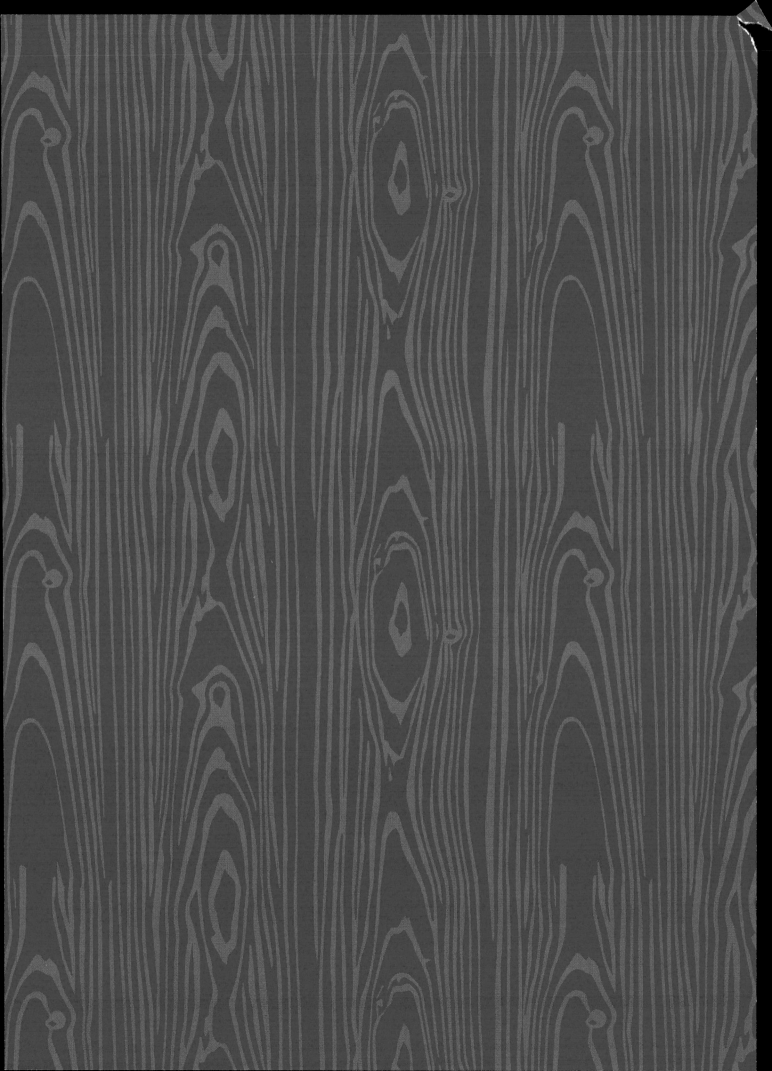

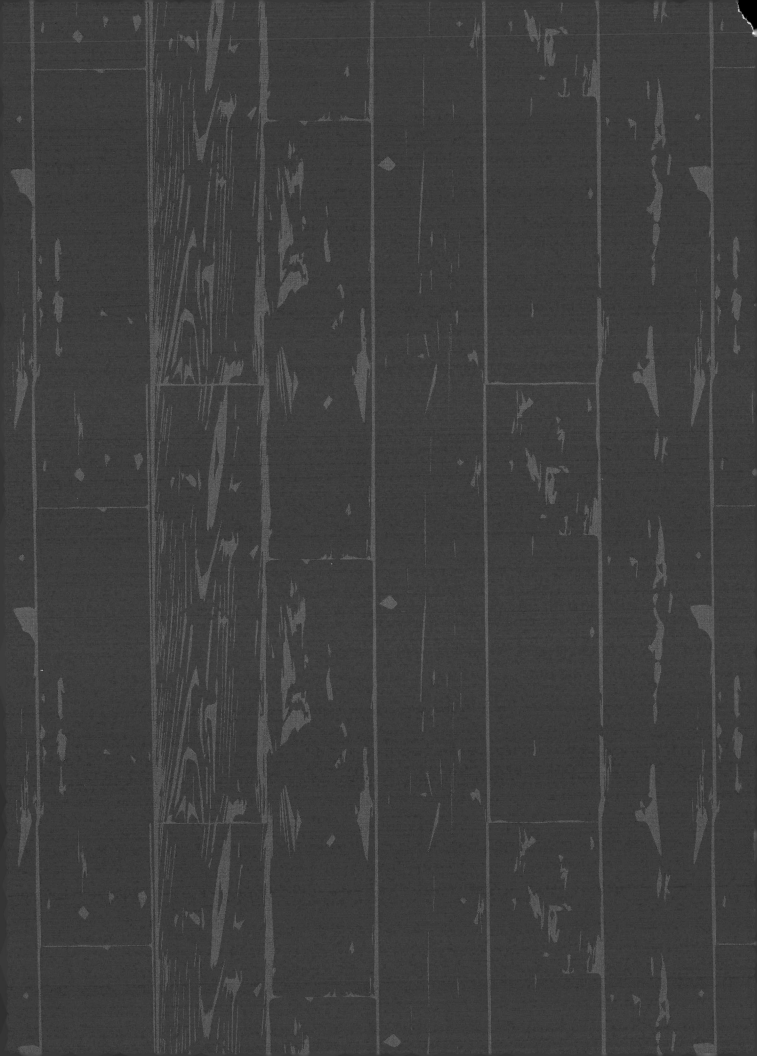

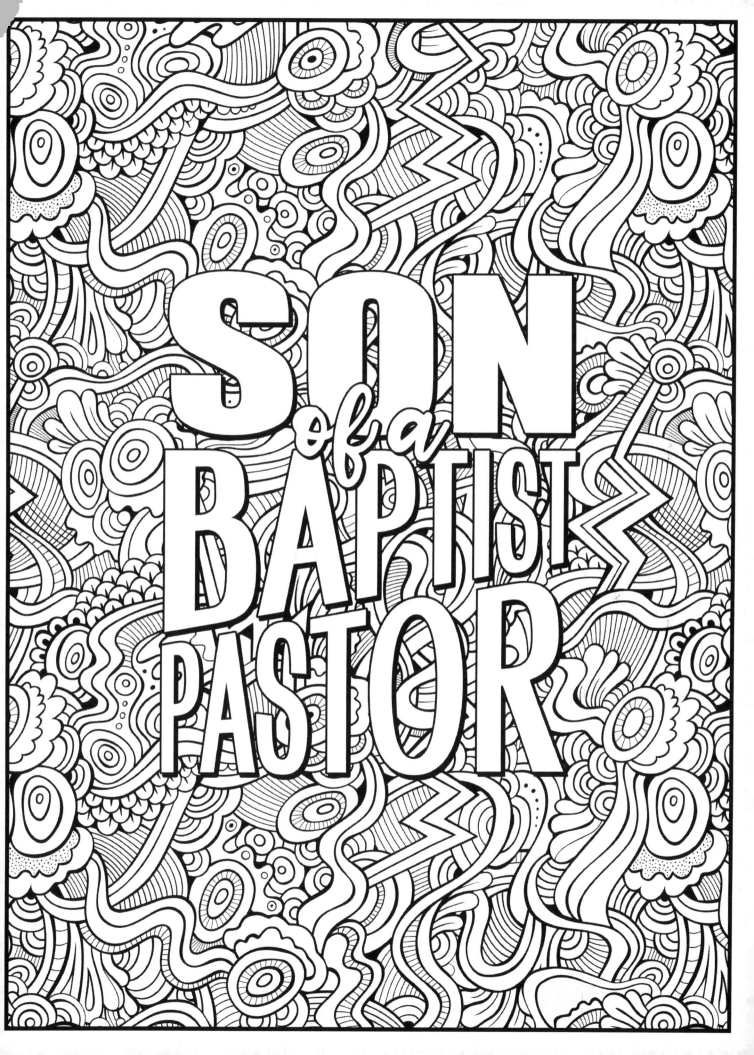

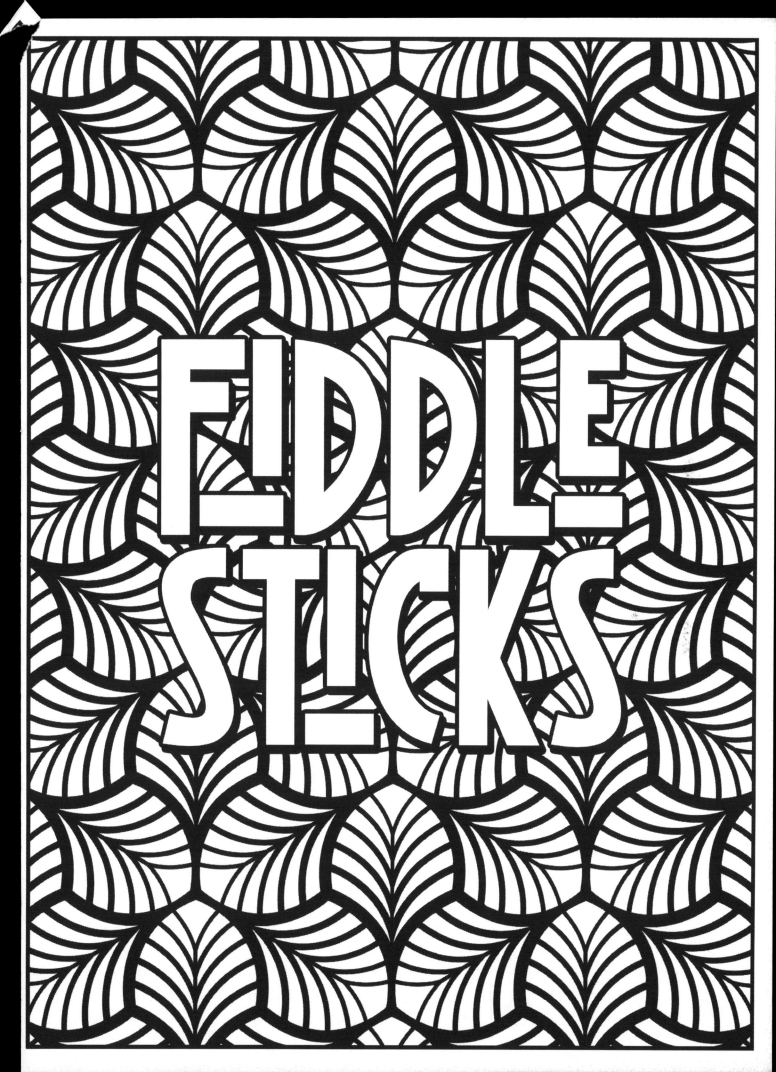

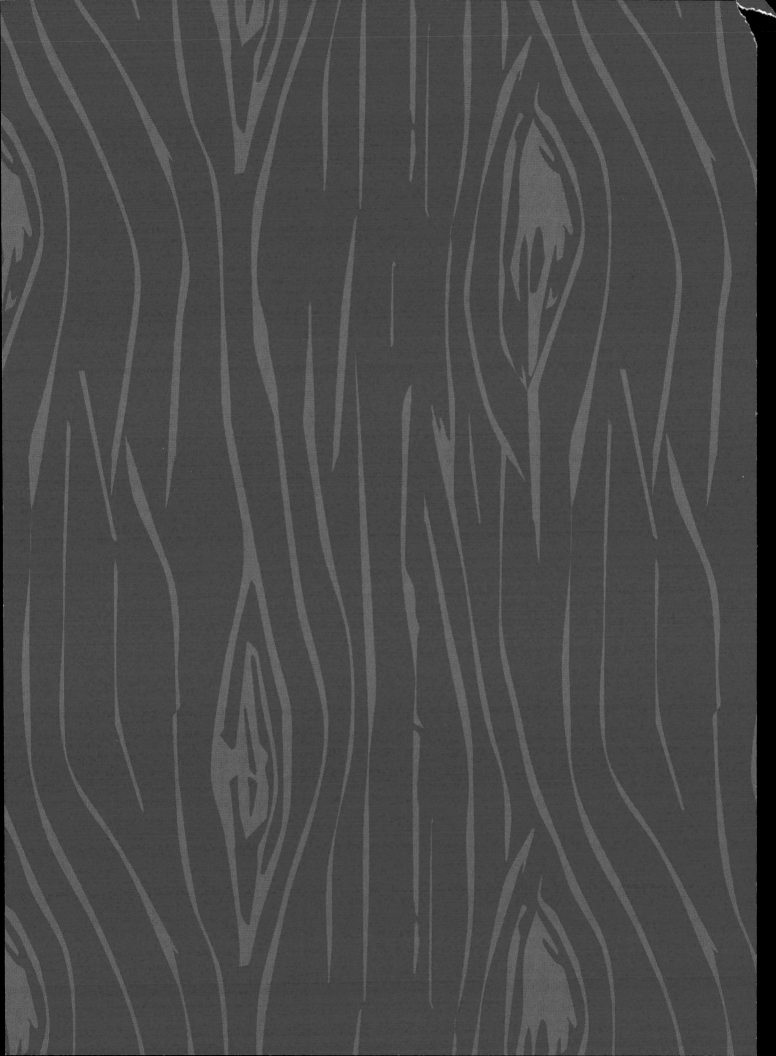

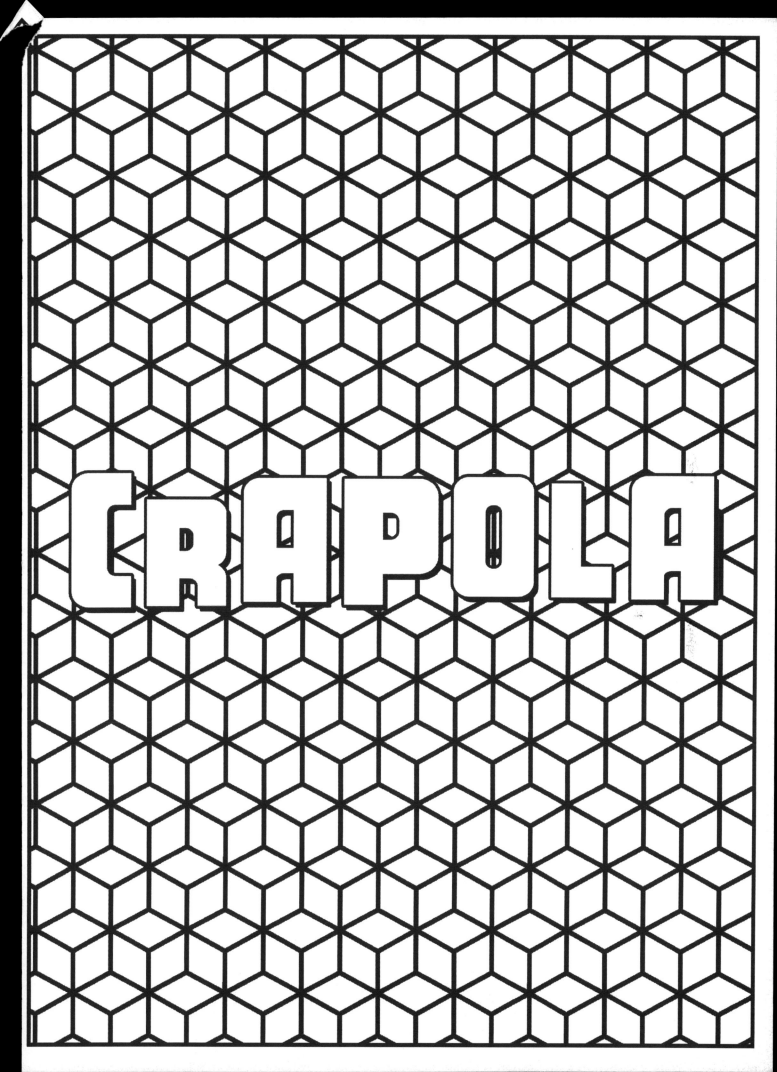

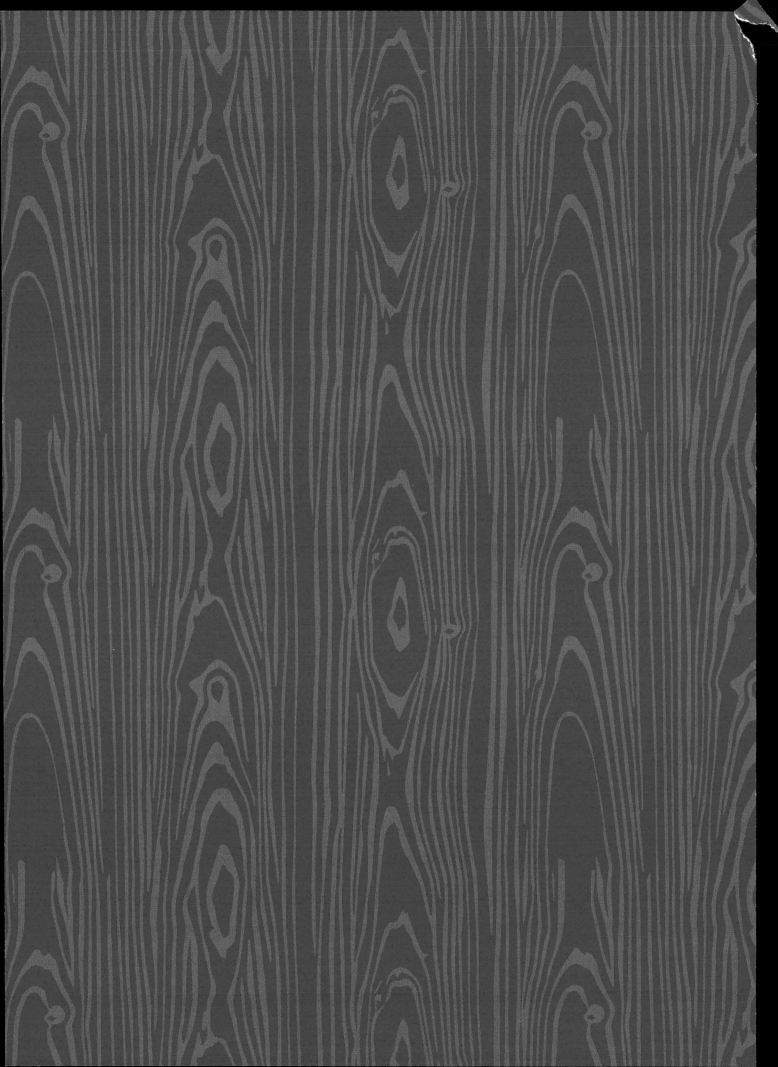

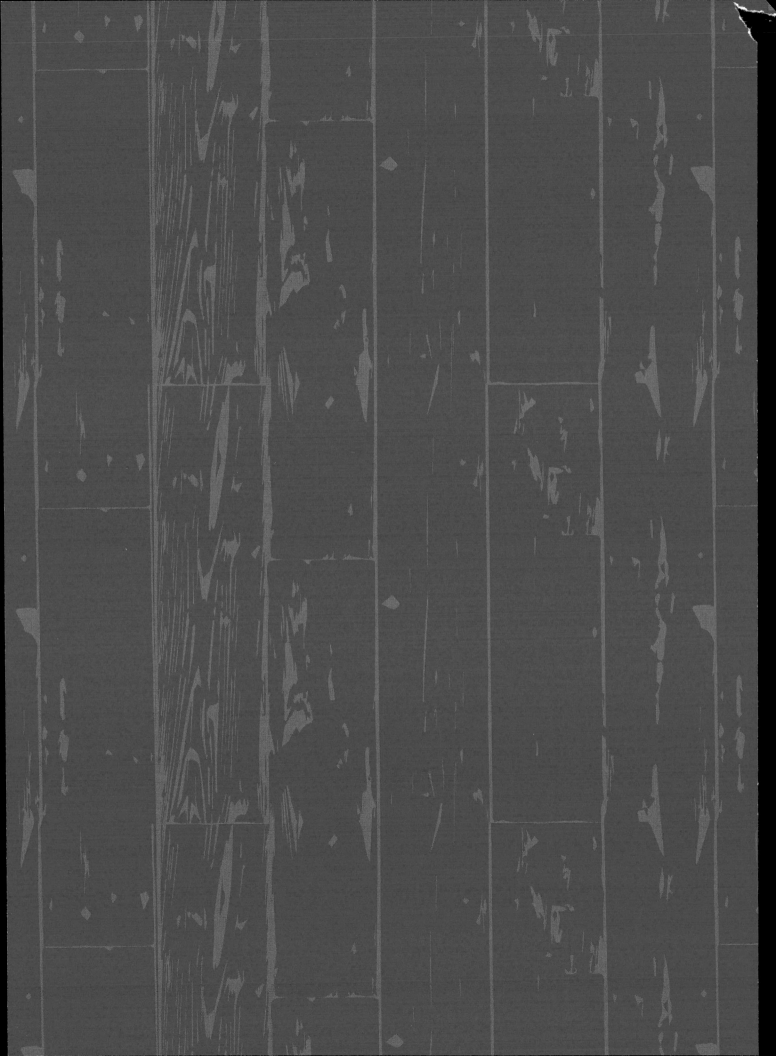

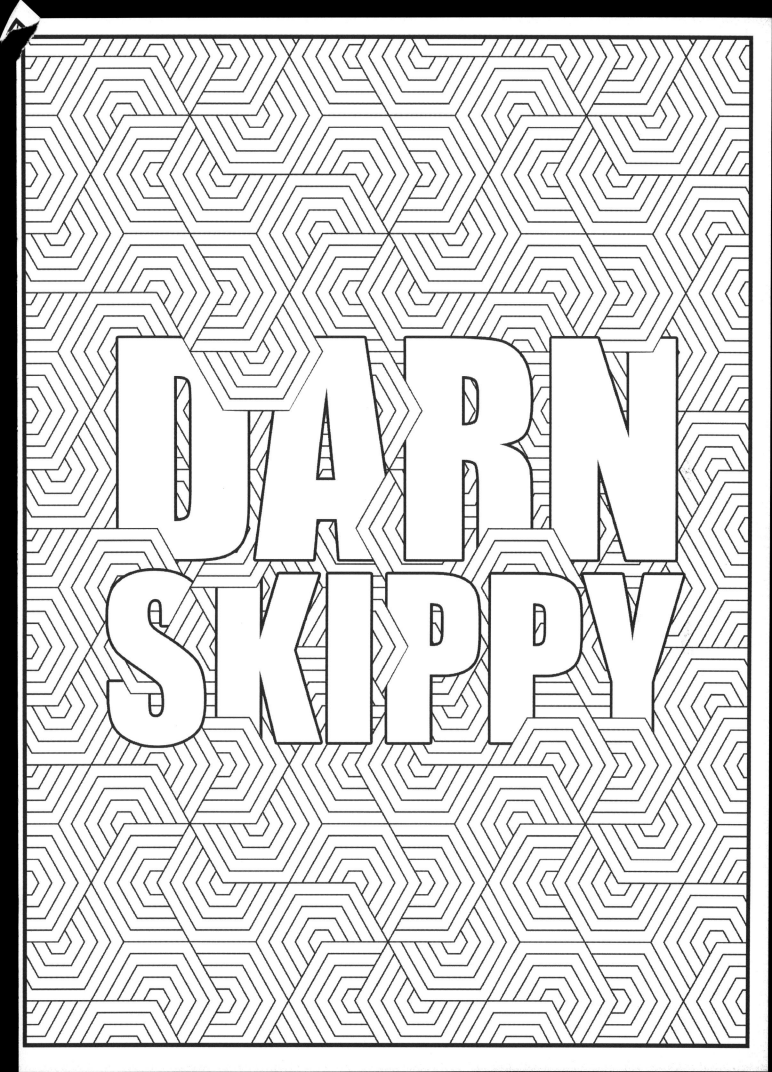

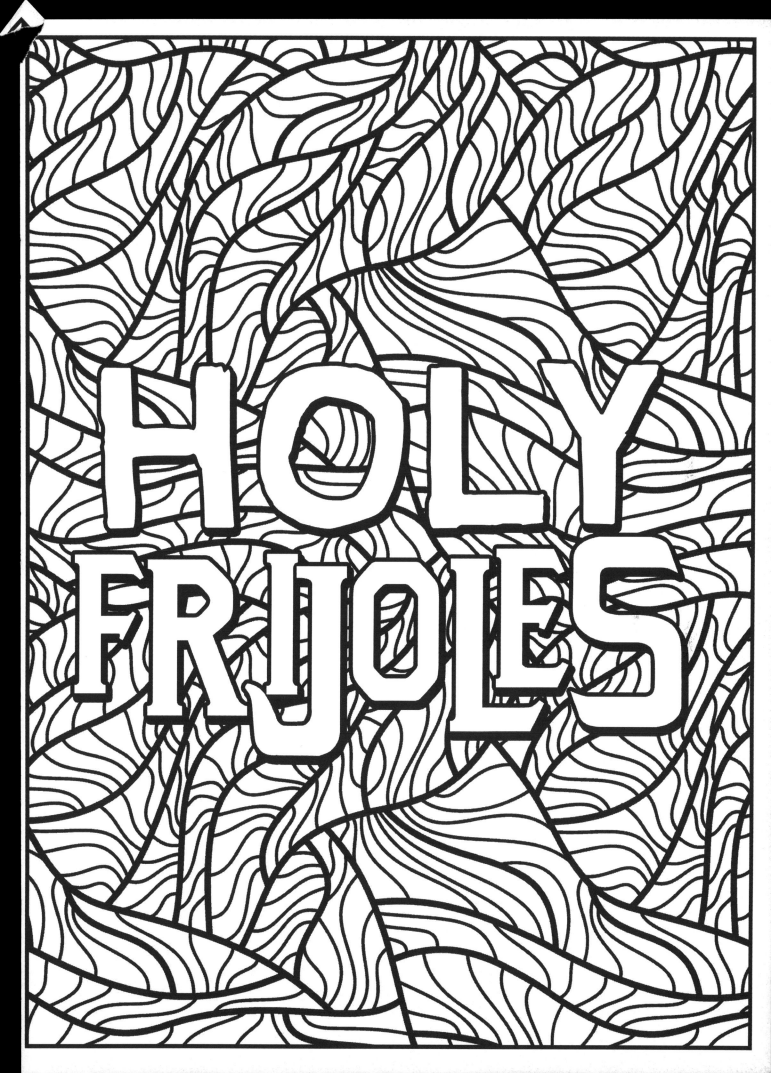

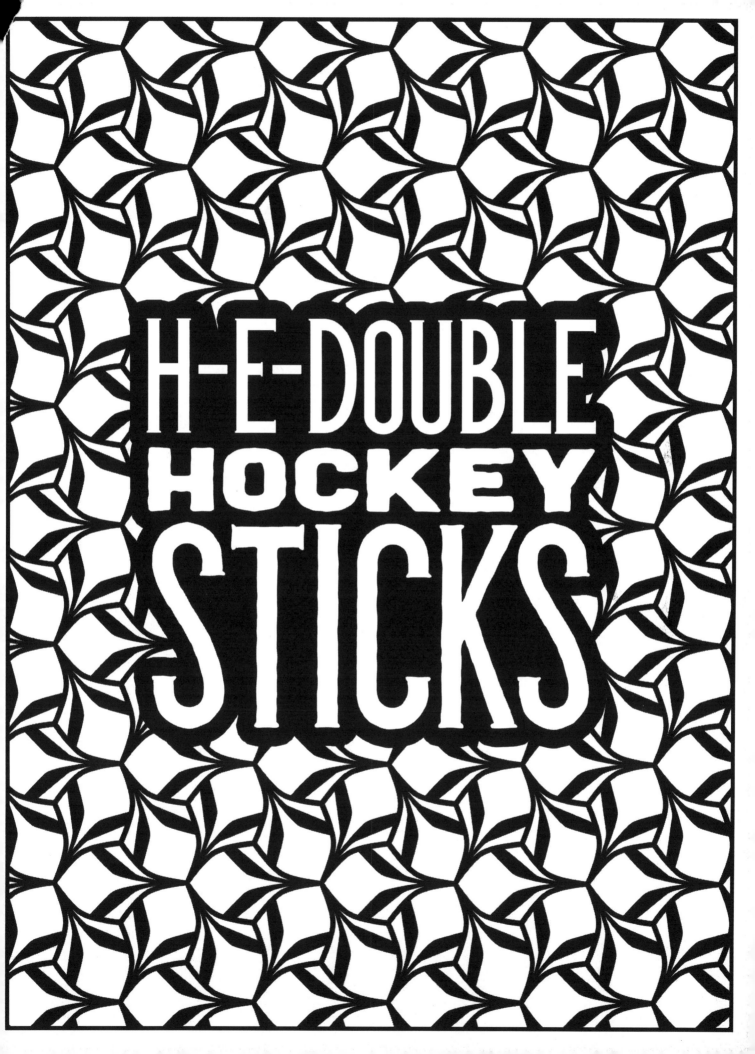

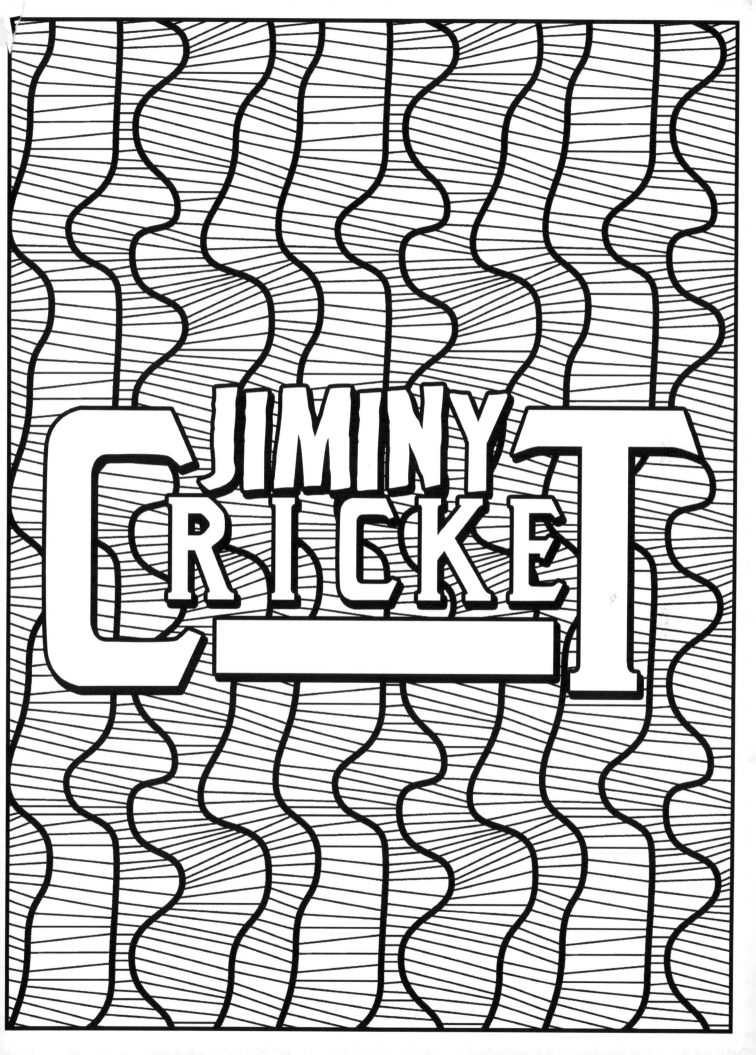

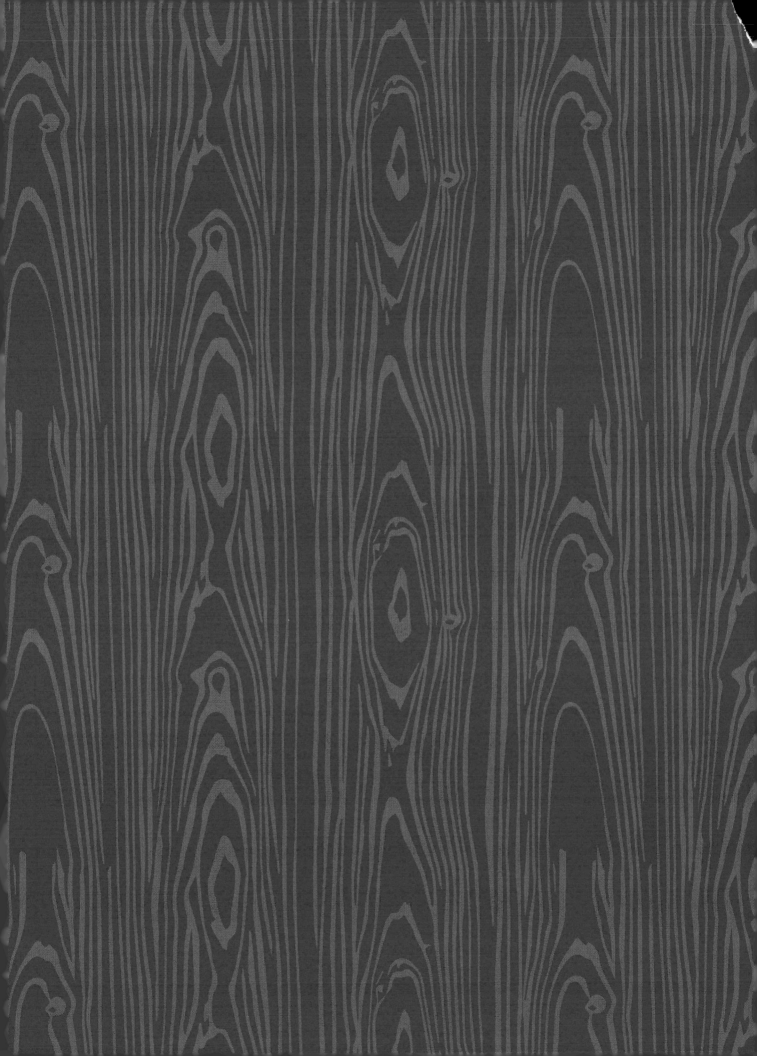

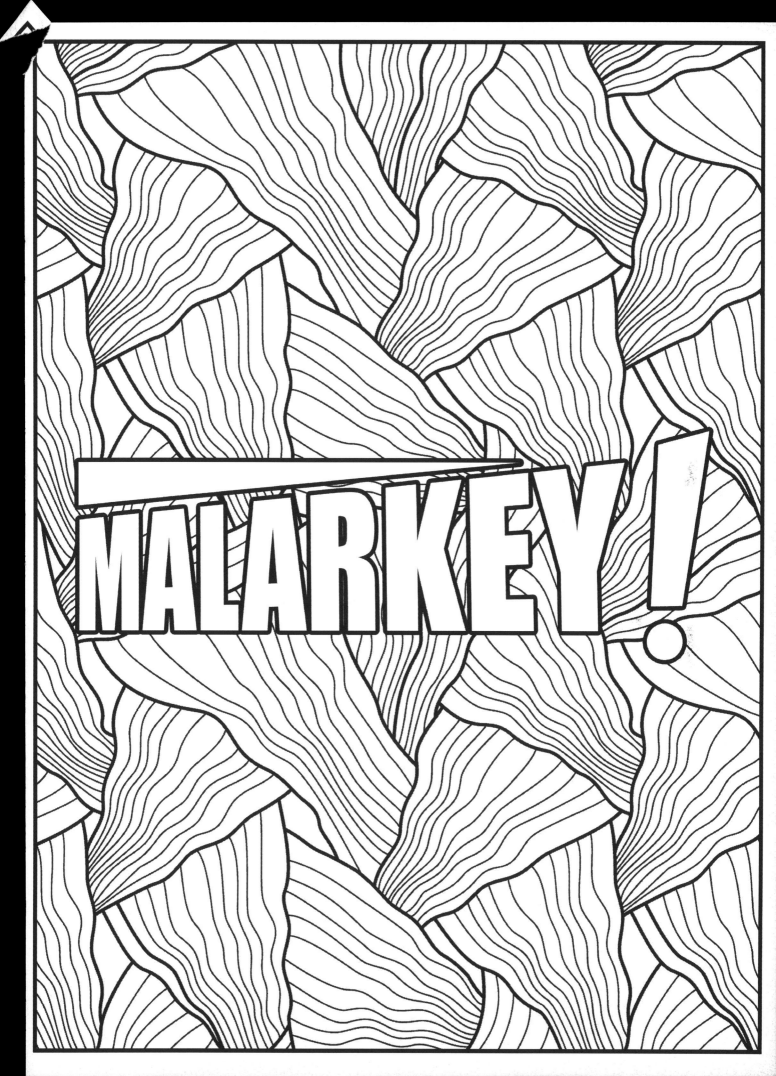

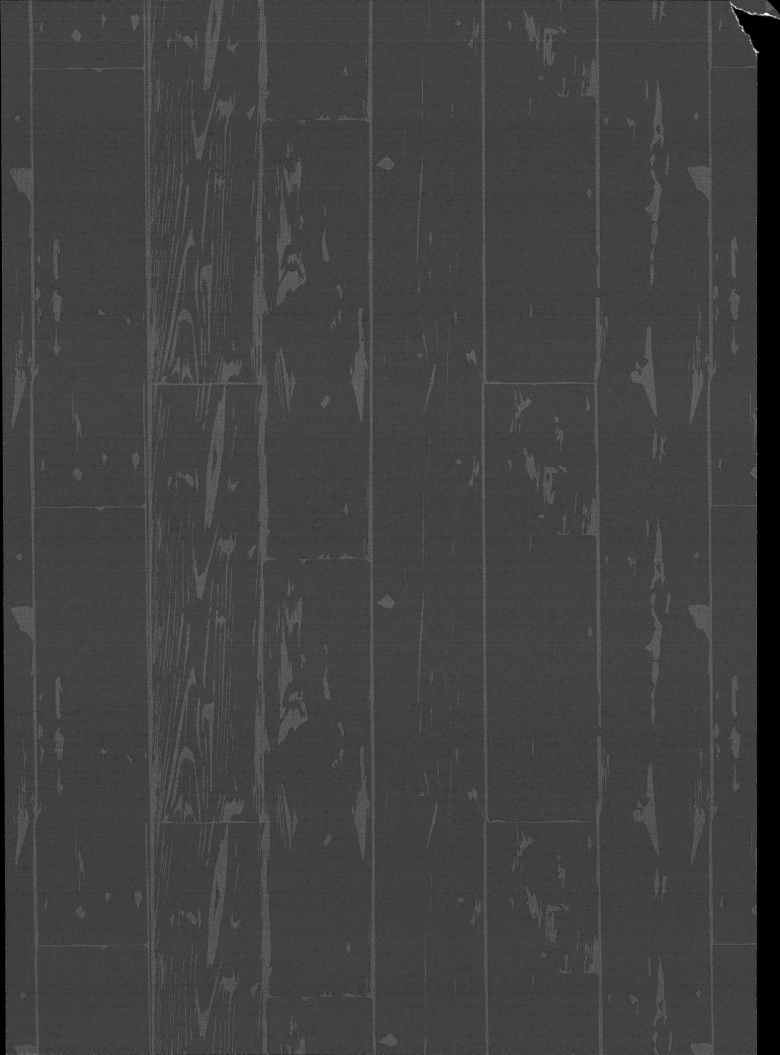

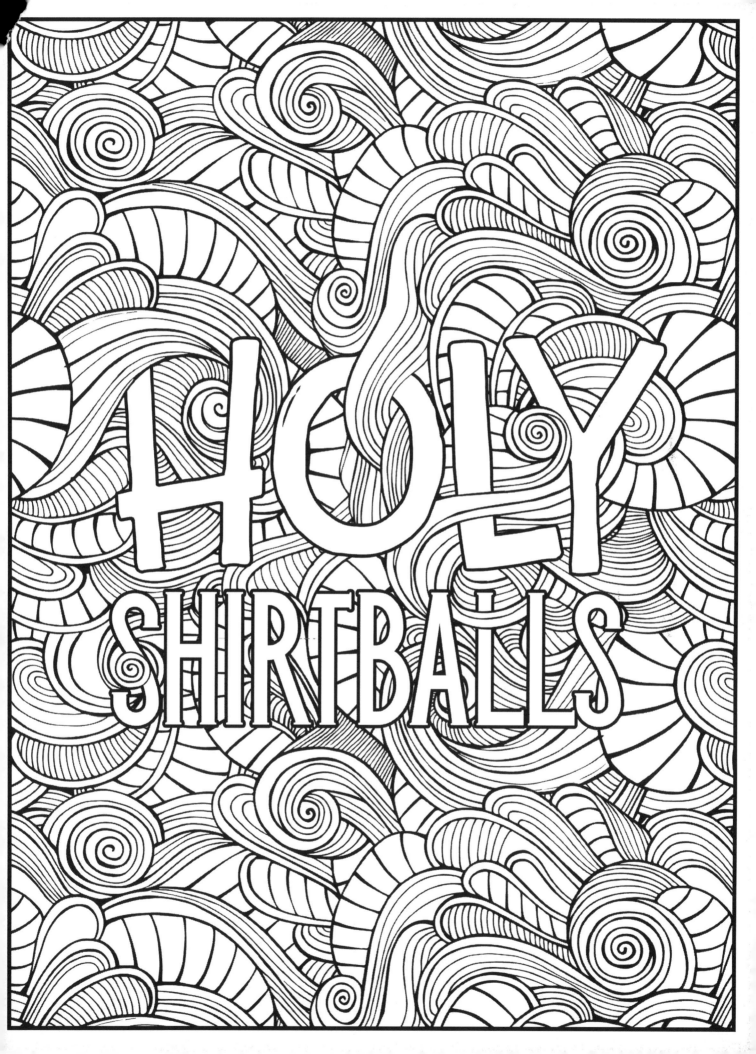

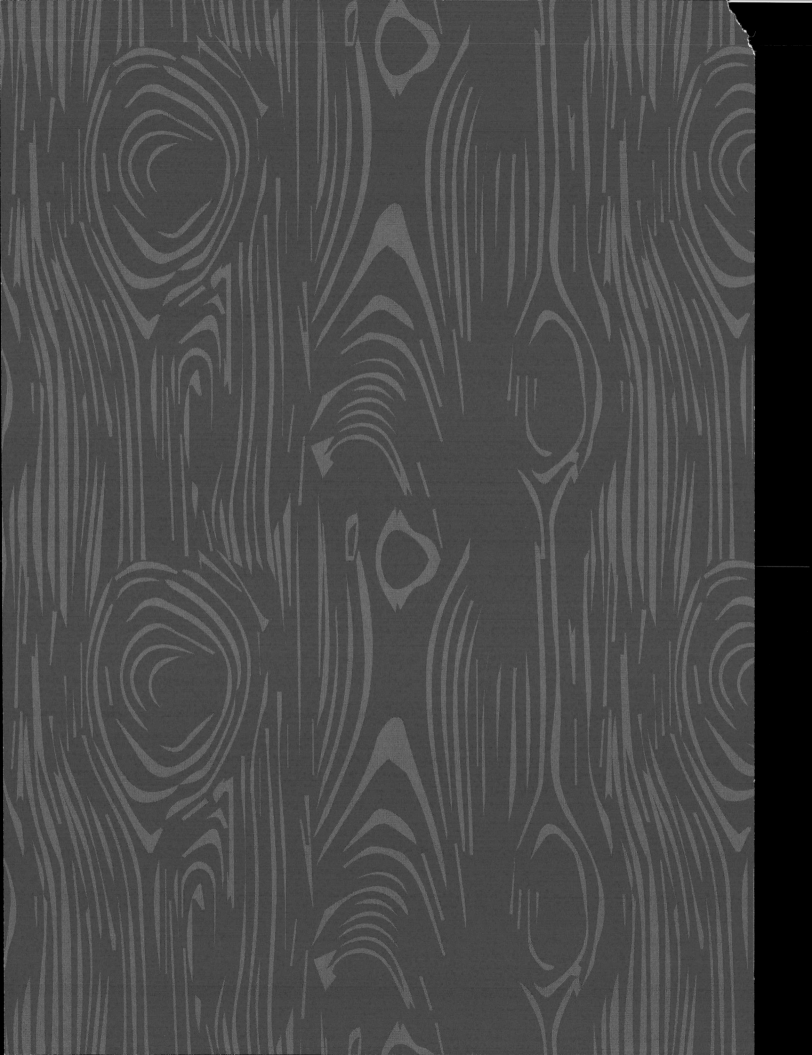

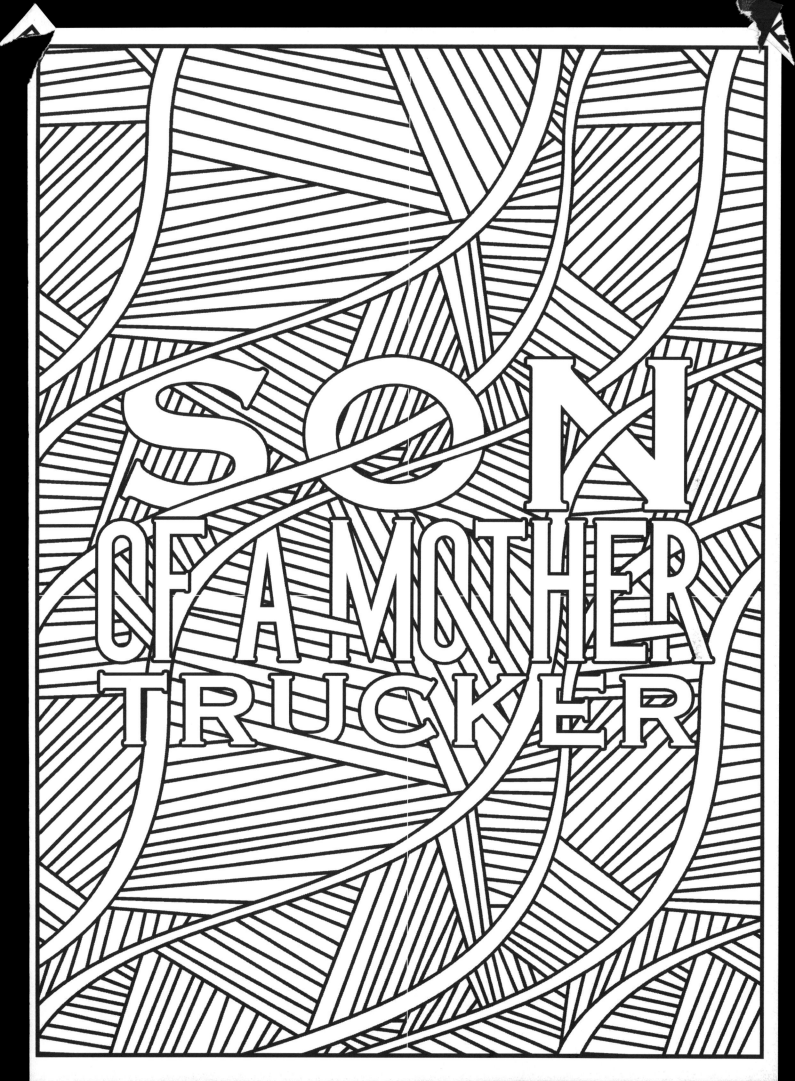

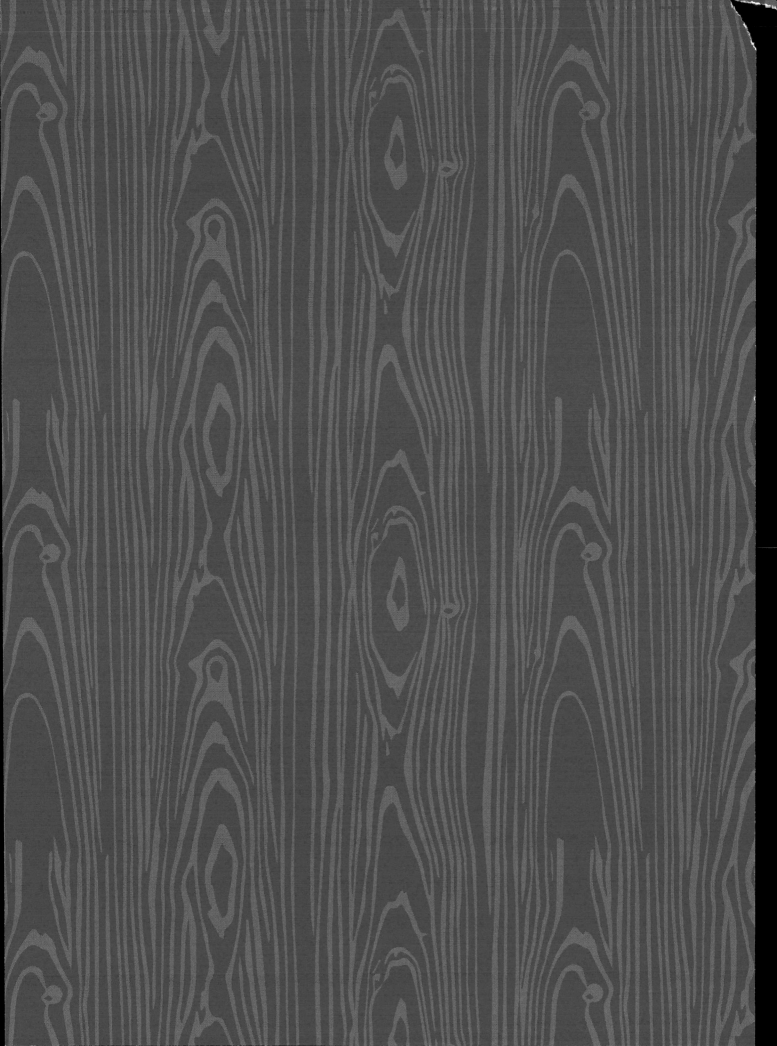

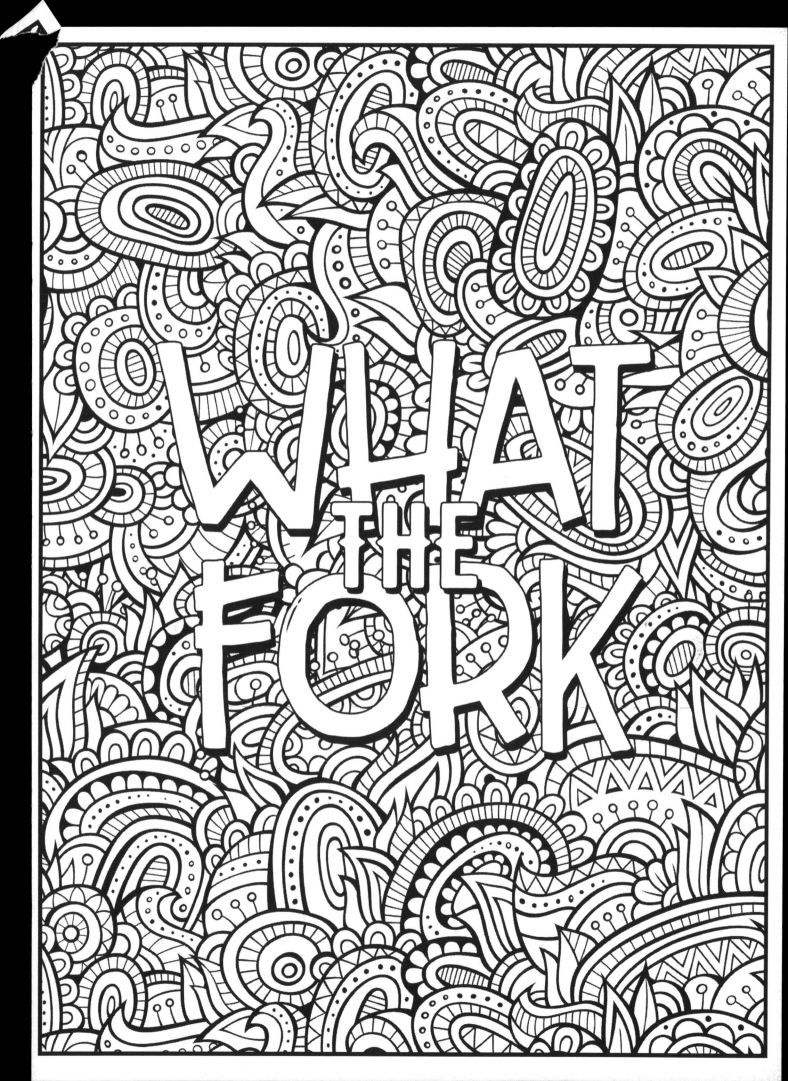

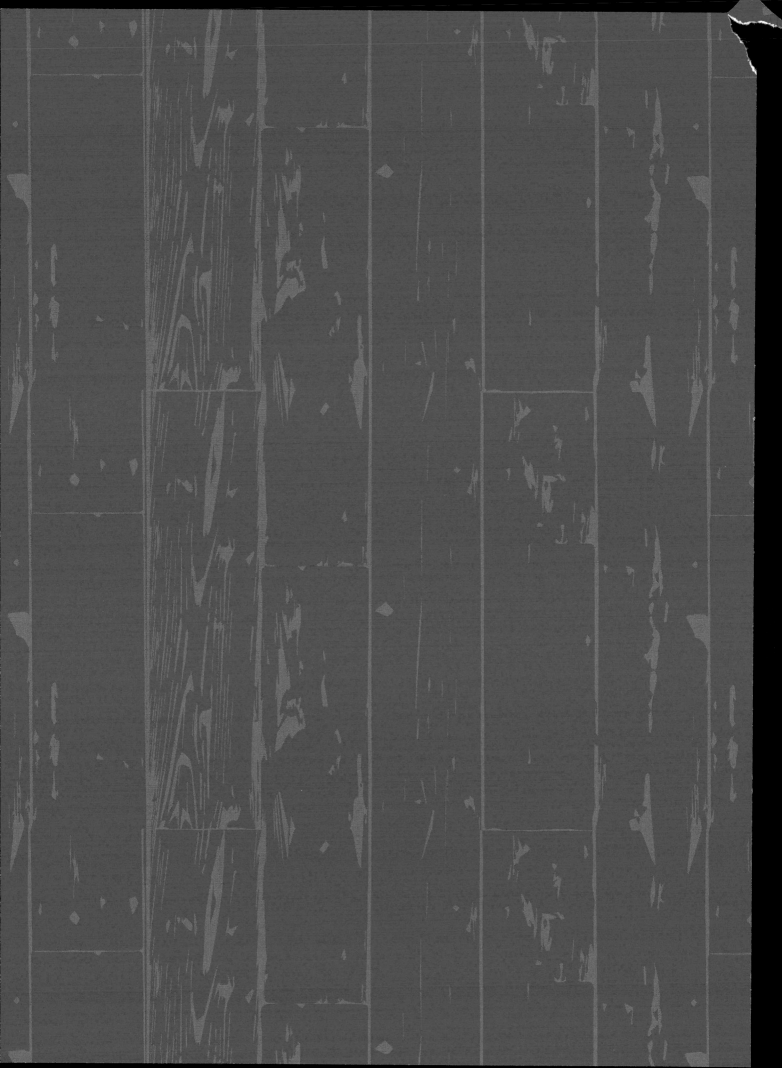

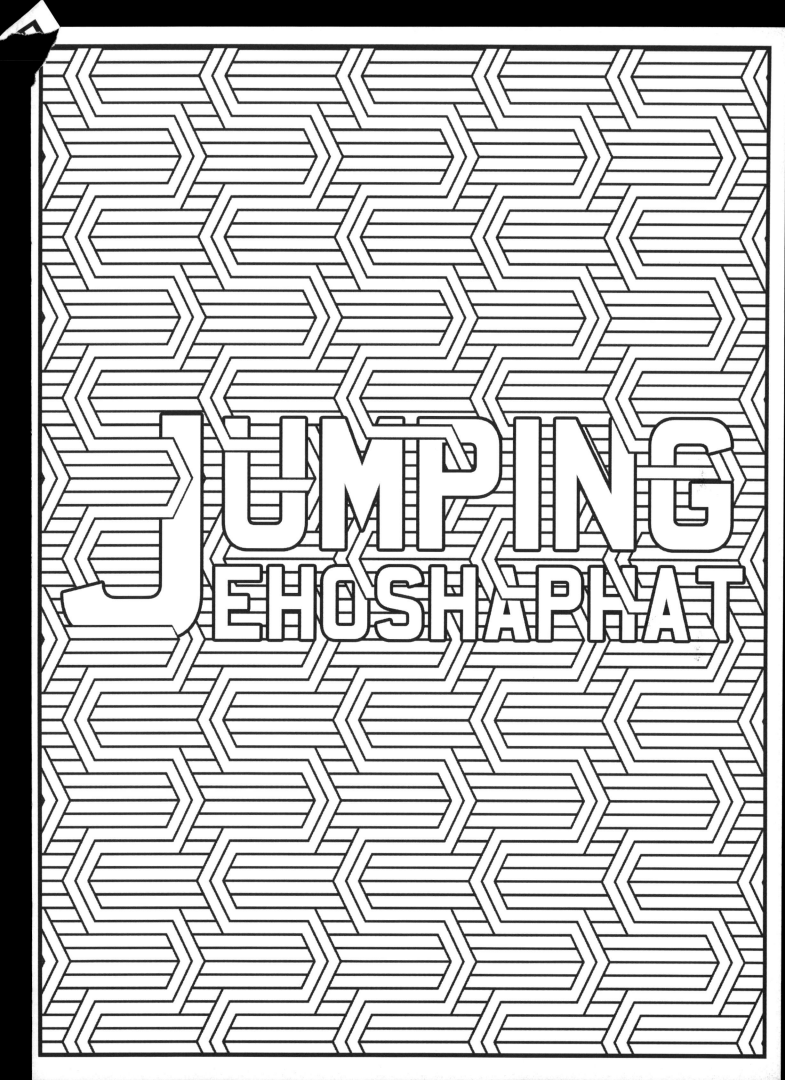

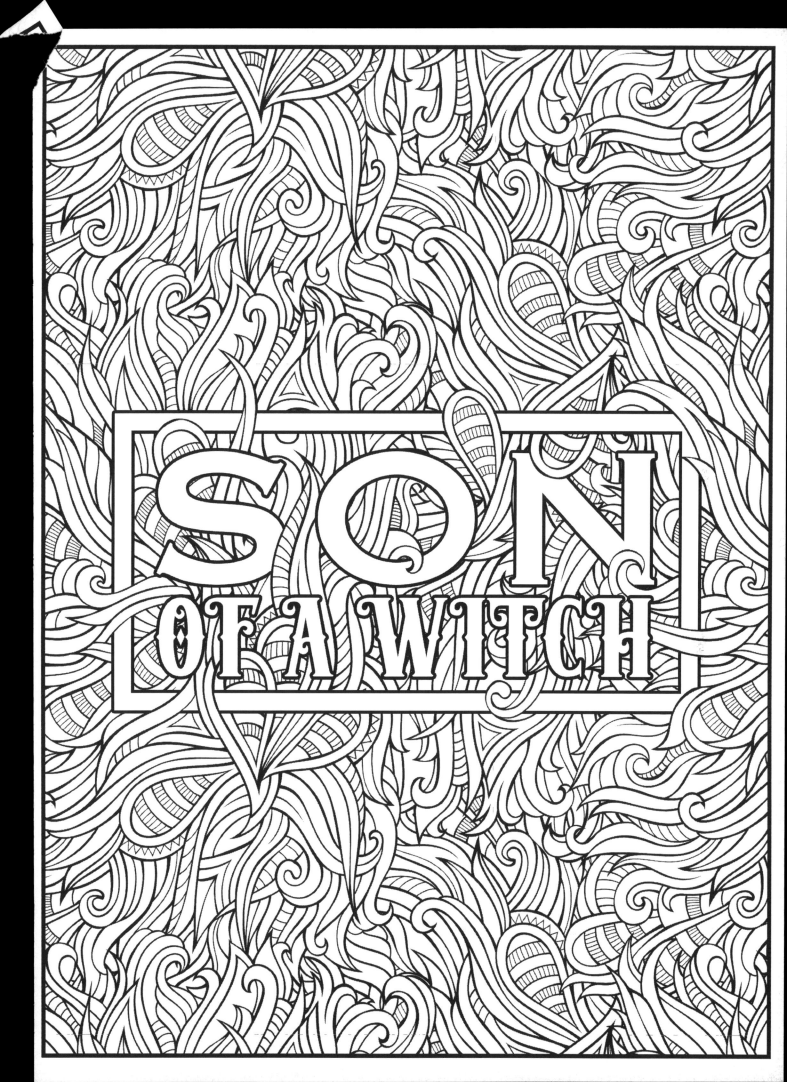

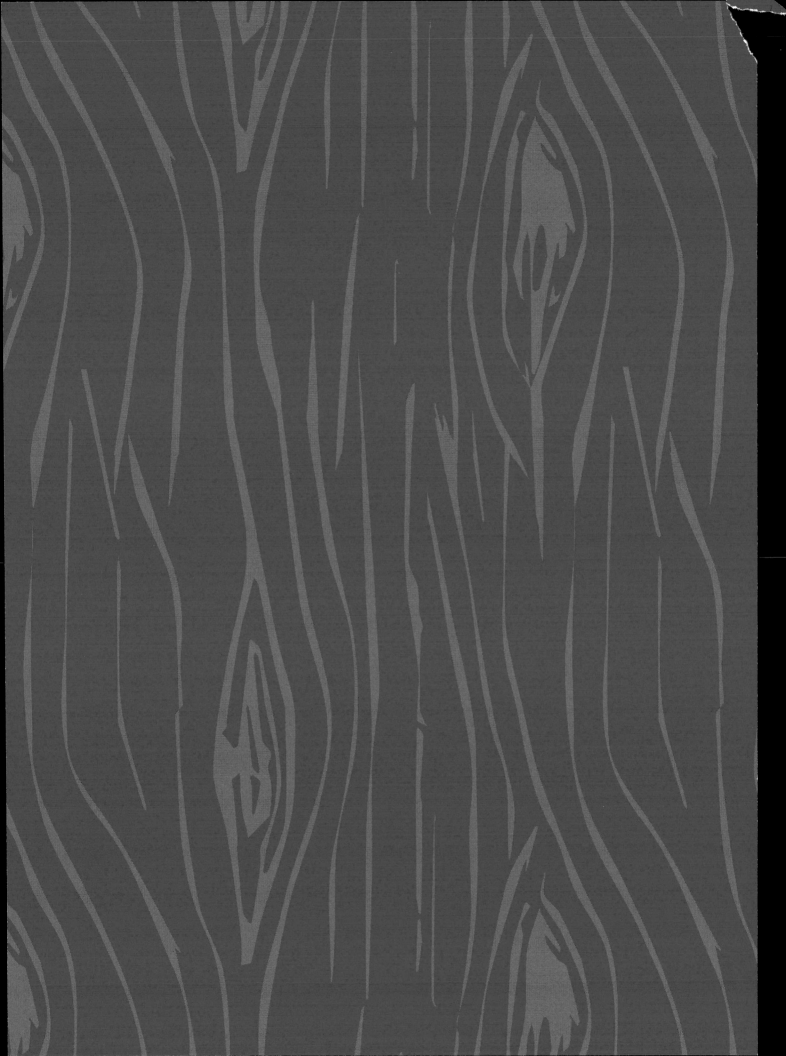

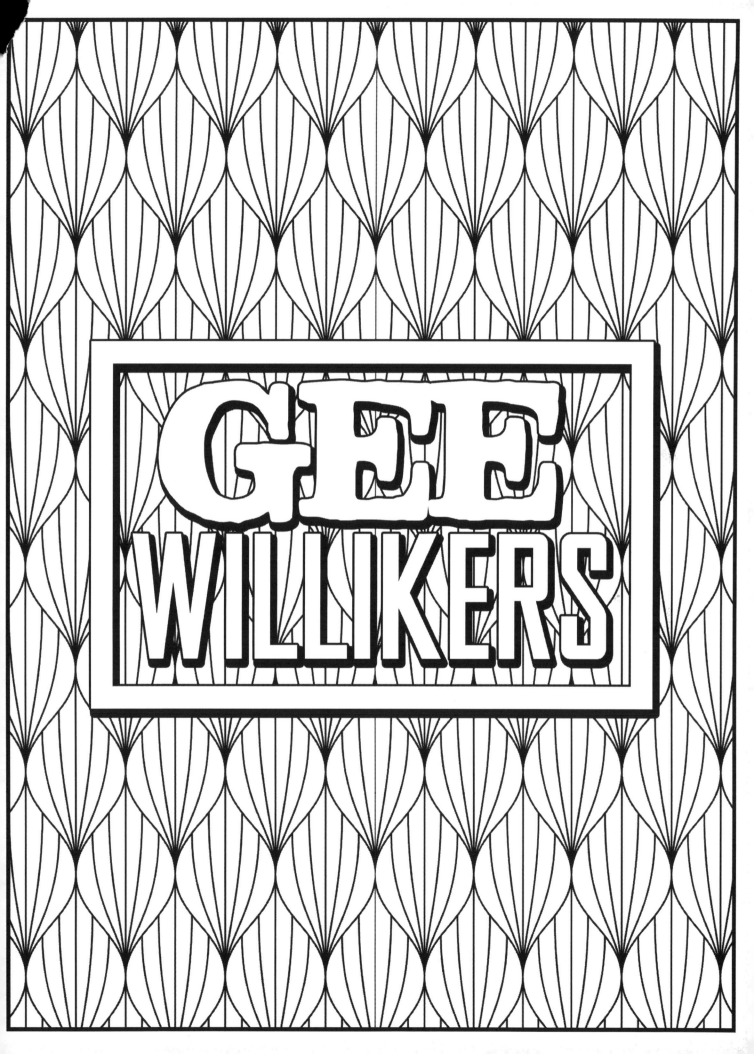

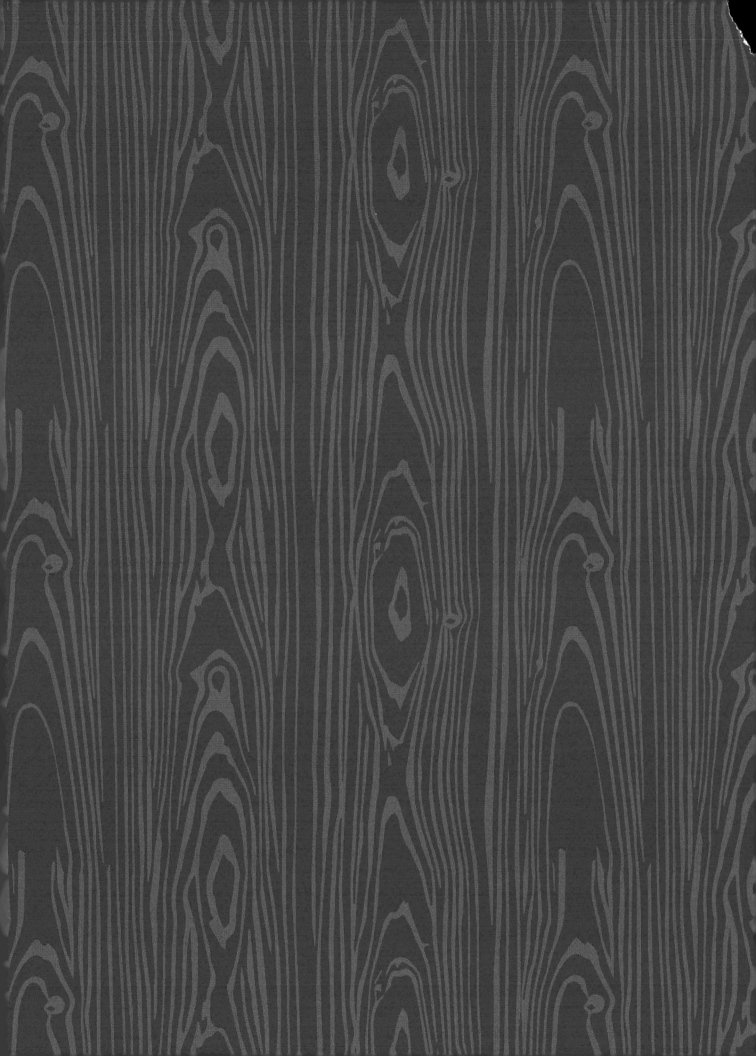

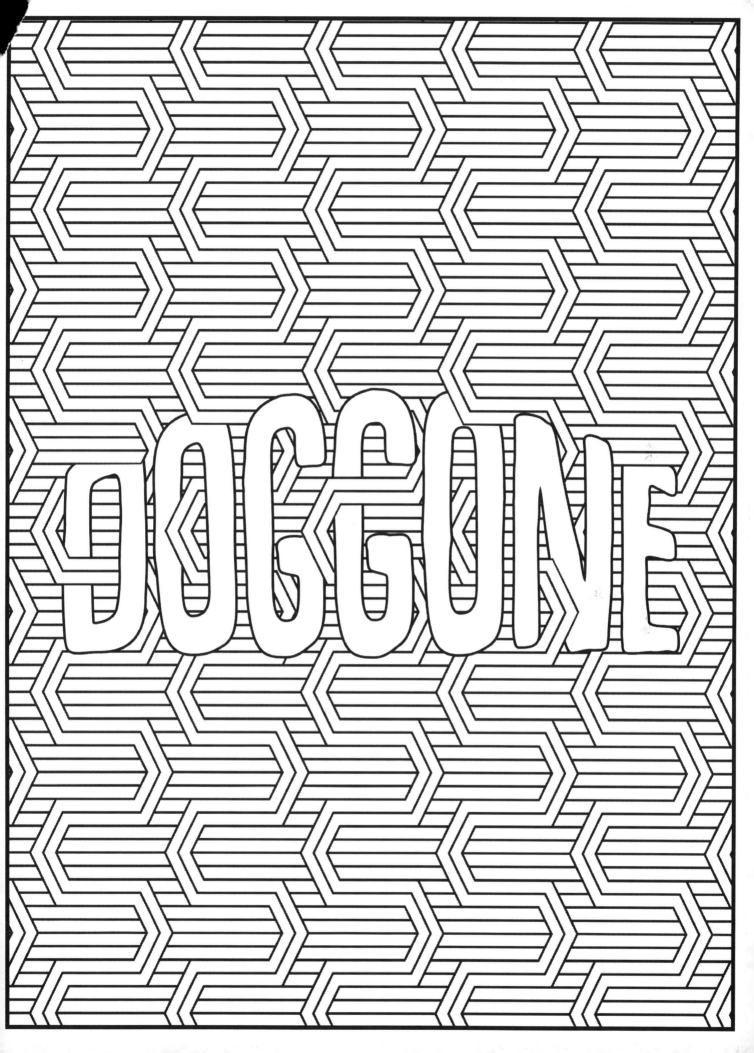

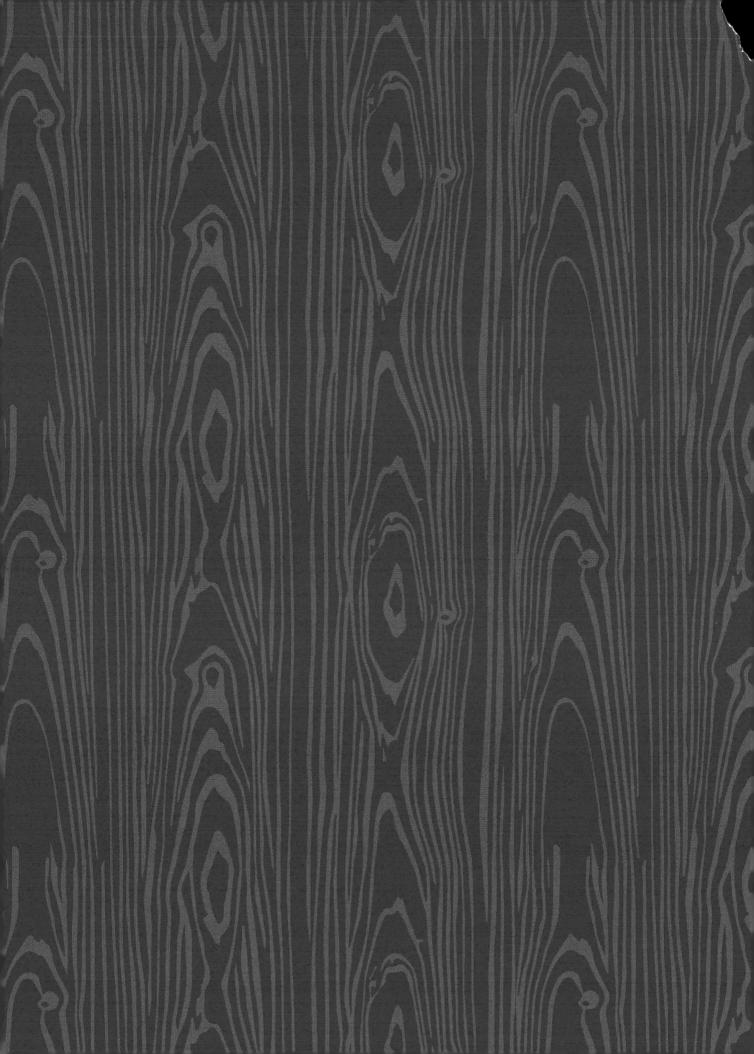

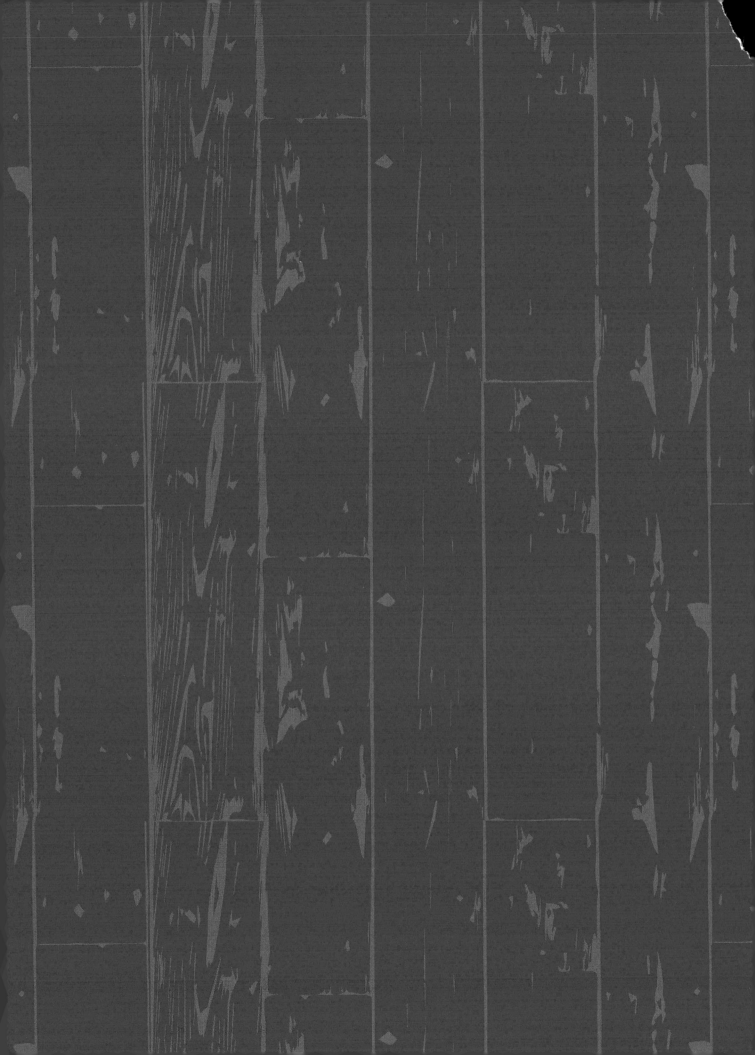

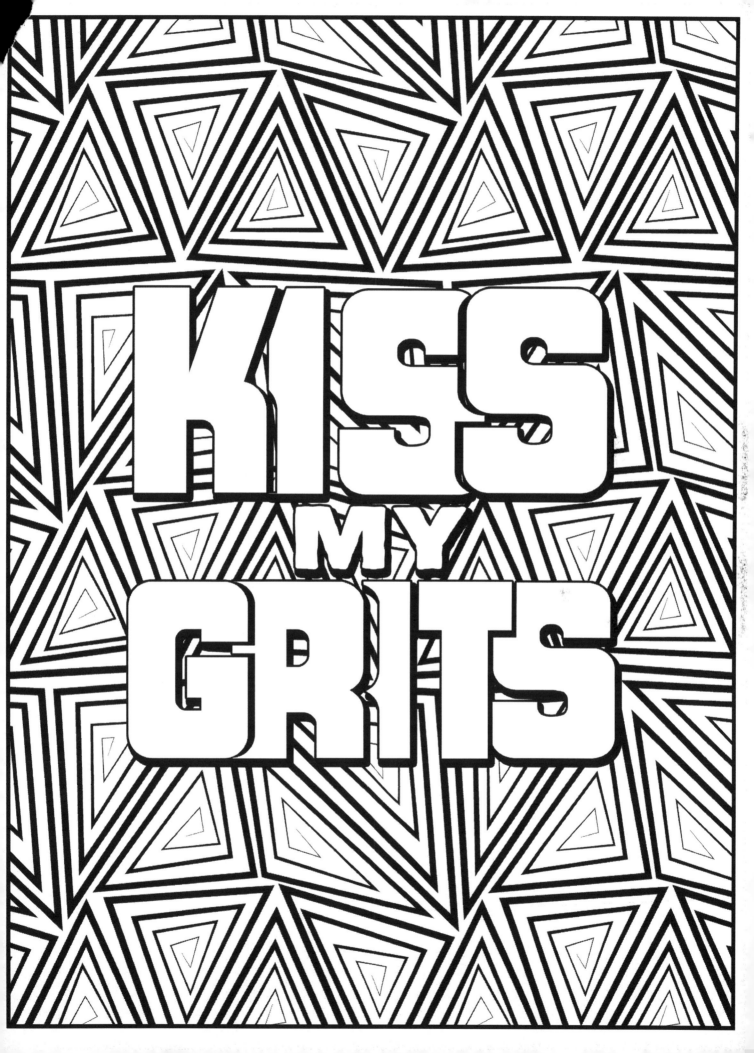

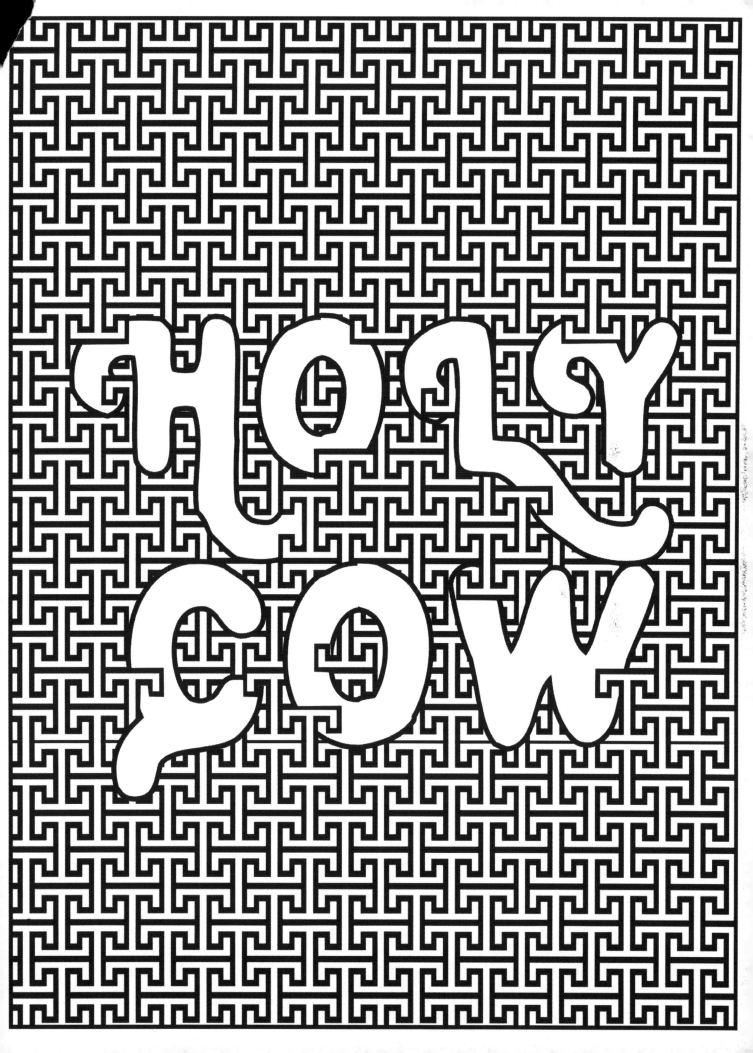

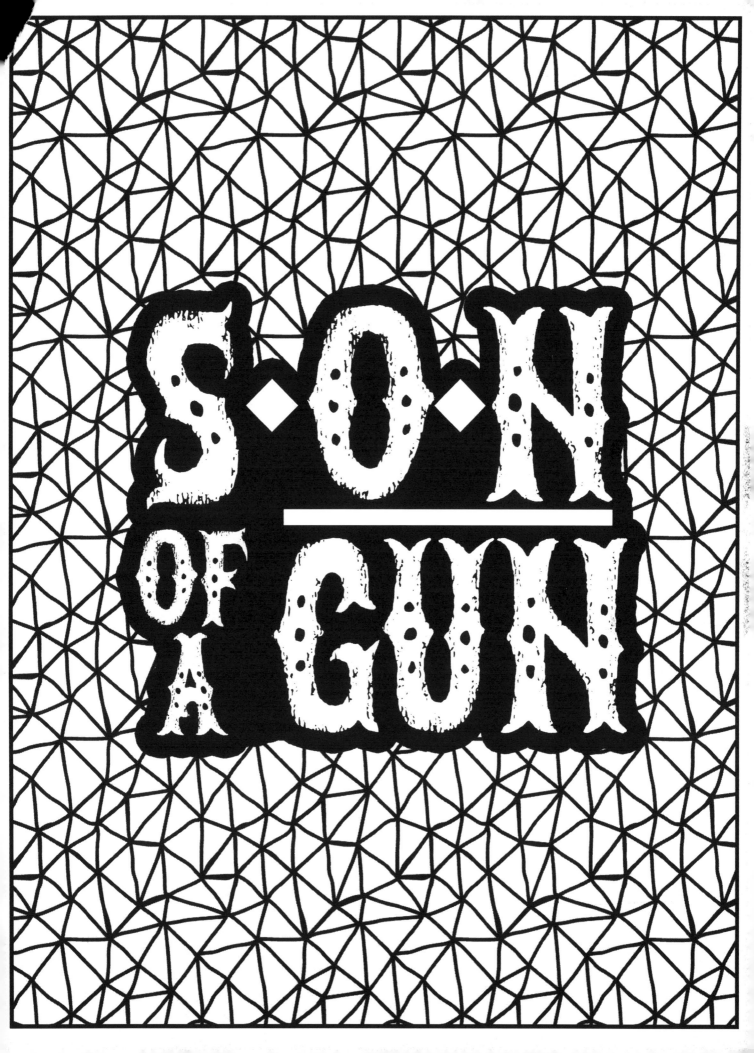

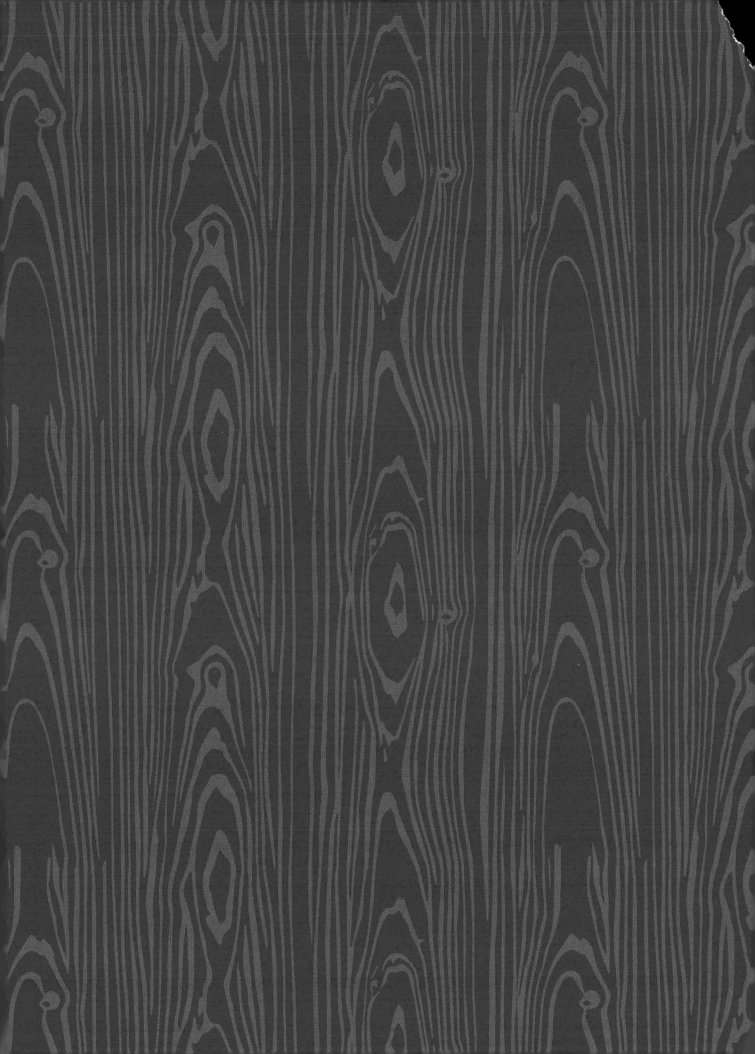

BE SURE TO FOLLOW US ON SOCIAL MEDIA FOR THE LATEST NEWS, SNEAK PEEKS, & GIVEAWAYS

[instagram icon] @PapeterieBleu

[facebook icon] Papeterie Bleu

[twitter icon] @PapeterieBleu

ADD YOURSELF TO OUR MONTHLY NEWSLETTER FOR FREE DIGITAL DOWNLOADS AND DISCOUNT CODES

www.papeteriebleu.com/newsletter

CHECK OUT OUR OTHER BOOKS!

www.papeteriebleu.com

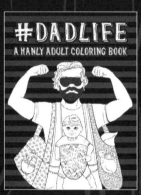
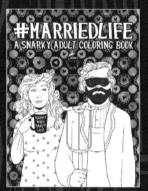

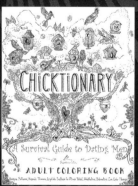

CHECK OUT OUR OTHER BOOKS!

www.papeteriebleu.com

CHECK OUT OUR OTHER BOOKS!

www.papeteriebleu.com

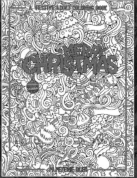

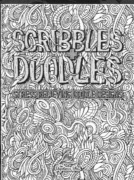
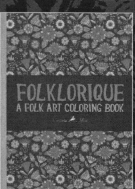

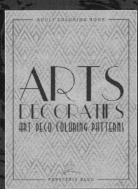

Made in the USA
Lexington, KY
26 February 2019